Apology for a Murder

Apology for a Murder

Lorenzino de' Medici

Translated by Andrew Brown

ET REMOTISSIMA PROPE

Hesperus Classics

Hesperus Classics
Published by Hesperus Press Limited
4 Rickett Street, London SW6 1RU
www.hesperuspress.com

Apology for a Murder first published in Italian as *Apologia* in 1539;
The Death of Lorenzino de' Medici first published in Italian as
L'ammazzamento di Lorenzino de' Medici in 1891
This translation first published by Hesperus Press Limited, 2004

Introduction and English language translation of *Apology for a Murder* and
The Death of Lorenzino de' Medici © Andrew Brown, 2004
English language translation of *Poems by Lorenzino de' Medici* © J.G. Nichols, 2004
Foreword © Tim Parks, 2004

Designed and typeset by Fraser Muggeridge
Printed in Italy by Graphic Studio Srl

ISBN: 1-84391-079-9

CONTENTS

What do you do if you come into the world bearing the same name as various ancestors, of whom some were considered good and others even great? Born in 1514, christened Lorenzo de' Medici, a young boy discovers that not only was his grandfather called Lorenzo, but likewise his great-great-grandfather, a man who is still revered as the good and generous brother of the even more revered Cosimo the Elder, who set up the Medici dynasty. Worst of all, there is the oppressive memory of Cosimo's grandson Lorenzo the Magnificent, whose posthumous fame is still growing despite the fact that he actually embezzled much of the wealth of your side of the family.

Well, one thing you can do is to call yourself something else. In general, Italian has two ways of altering a word or name. There is the affectionate diminutive produced by the suffix *-ino*, and the insulting pejorative created by the suffix *-accio*. Hence we have *ragazzo*, a boy, *ragazzino*, a nice little boy, and *ragazzaccio*, a young hooligan. Curiously, Lorenzo came to be known both as Lorenzino, perhaps because he was short, perhaps because it was understood that he was bound to be less important than his ancestor namesakes, and Lorenzaccio, 'nasty Lorenzo'. Quite probably he got this second name because of the way he reacted to the implications of the first.

Orphaned young, Lorenzino went down to Rome to live under the guardianship of Pope Clement VII, illegitimate son of Lorenzo the Magnificent's brother, and hence a man on the other, embezzling side of the family. This was now very much the heyday of the Renaissance, after a century bent on redis-covering the noble gestures, artworks and writings of the ancient world, largely at the expense of the medieval Christian

values of humility, poverty and chastity.

The constant search for role models in ancient Rome and Greece, and in particular the tendency to judge political leaders by comparing them with famous figures of antiquity, had a variety of consequences, positive and negative. Certainly there was an enhanced sense of human nobility, of a greatness and beauty that could be achieved and contemplated aside from Christian metaphysics. But there was also the danger of falling into parody, or cynicism, of feeling that every action was merely the tired repetition – and what's more, out of context – of something done centuries before. On a wild night in 1530 the adolescent Lorenzino went out and vandalised the bas-reliefs on the Emperor Constantine's triumphal arch, plus various fine statues from the age of Hadrian. Was this destructive act a rejection of the encumbering past, or was Lorenzino mimicking Alcibiades, who had supposedly mutilated various busts of Hermes almost two thousand years before? In any event the young Medici was obliged to abandon Rome on pain of death. Fleeing to Florence, he wrote a play, the *Aridosio*, which begins with the complaint that it is impossible to find anything new to write about because the ancients have already done it all.

Florence at the time was itself enjoying a collective déjà vu. After a period of republicanism, the Pope and the Holy Roman Emperor had got together to impose, once again, a Medici leadership on the city. Alessandro de' Medici, bastard son, so it seemed, of Pope Clement VII, was declared Duke. Poor but resourceful, Lorenzino befriended his distant cousin – Alessandro was only four years his senior – and became his companion in debauchery, an able procurer of women, an adviser, a buffoon, a heavy drinker. Then, at a certain point, he decided to kill him. 'My beautiful aunt,' he told Alessandro one

night in 1537, 'is at last ready to grant you her favours. You can wait for her in my bedroom.' Alessandro rose to the bait. He lay down on his cousin's bed and shut his eyes. Together with a hired assassin, Lorenzino, now decidedly Lorenzaccio, stabbed him to death and fled before the body was discovered.

Why did he do it? There appears to have been no plan and certainly no proper preparation for replacing the Duke with either himself or the prominent republicans whom Alessandro had exiled. In the *Apology* Lorenzino sets out to explain. The things to look for as you read the piece are the passion and elegance of its arguments, the ease with which internal contradiction is ignored, the insistent sincerity of its false consciousness, and the fact that at the end of the day nothing at all is really explained.

Life is only worth living if man is free, Lorenzino begins, therefore tyrannicide is a duty. The ancients always said as much. The Florentines know it in their republican blood. Alessandro was worse than Nero and Caligula put together. It's amazing it took so long for someone to find the courage to be rid of him. The implication is that the author himself is a modern Brutus.

Up to this point the piece is no more than a vehement repetition of the principles of Roman republicanism, an exercise in finding parallels in the ancient past. But then Lorenzino enters into a fine discussion of the whole question of the legitimacy of political power. Surprisingly now, he doesn't take a doctrinaire republican position. He is flexible. Traditionally, Florence has belonged to its people, not to a hereditary Duke. But even if it were conceded that the Holy Roman Emperor had the right to impose a leader on Florence, Alessandro would have forfeited any hypothetical legitimacy with his appallingly cruel and licentious behaviour. For what

really gives a government the right to rule is its performance.

All this seems admirable and sensibly pragmatic. There is a discussion of Lorenzino's obligations to a member of his extended family with whom he was in a close relationship. Here he oscillates wonderfully between his supposed commitment to republicanism, which would have obliged him to kill a tyrant even if it were his own brother, and a sense of social superiority in being the true legitimate son of a Medici and not merely a bastard fathered on a serving maid by God knows who. But in any event, since the end justifies the means (Lorenzino was clearly familiar with Machiavelli's *The Prince*, published some twenty years before), then his treacherous exploitation of his special relationship with Alessandro is more than excusable: the important thing was to kill the pig.

This discussion of ends and means leads us to the core of the *Apology* and its underlying irony. For the goal of the whole project, Lorenzino claims, was to return Florence to its republican constitution. This end failed, he complains, because the people who should have risen up on the announcement of the Duke's death were so pusillanimous. The question now arises: is the means justified if the end is not achieved? And we see that Machiavelli's famous precept introduces an element of technical expertise into morality: only a correct calculation of the consequences of any action will allow us to understand whether it is morally justified. Lorenzino got it wrong. He killed Alessandro, but this led only to the installation of another Medici, Cosimo I, as Duke. That was definitely not the plan. All the same, the murderer claims the justification of his intended end, which only he could really know and which, as we have said, he does not seem to have planned or provided for in any serious way.

What, then, are the intentions behind the *Apology* itself? At

first glance the text seems to be a genuine political treatise and an attempt to win support, perhaps the preparation for a possible return to Florence. But Lorenzino could not have been so foolish as to have imagined that the ruling Medici would ever forgive him. He knew there were paid assassins forever on his track as he moved nervously from town to town. So what was the purpose of this eloquent piece of writing? Like the destruction of the statues in Rome, the writing of his play, the assassination of the Duke, it can best be seen as just another attempt to achieve fame. This was Lorenzino's real goal, the only explanation. He wanted to be noticed.

At this point the relevance of the *Apology* to our own times becomes evident. Renaissance humanism, with its combination of eclecticism and stress on the noble individual, offered a gallery of gestures, usually bereft of context, that would lead to fame. After centuries of a Christianity that allowed for nothing outside itself, the door was opened on the supermarket of ideas and role models we live in today. From now on modern man could invest in this or that role to achieve notoriety, not because he believed in it, but because he believed he was capable of distinguishing himself in this way. At which point everybody begins to insist on their sincerity, precisely because we sense its absence. Immoral and aristocratic, Lorenzino de' Medici becomes famous writing a work of great morality and enthusiastic republicanism. The nineteenth-century poet Giacomo Leopardi would refer to the *Apology* as the best prose writing of its time. The fact that we are reading Lorenzino today is an indication of his triumph.

Then in 1548 the hired killers caught up with him in Venice. To read, immediately after the *Apology*, Francesco Bibboni's colourful account of how he and an accomplice dispatched Lorenzino, is to find oneself at the opposite pole of literary

INTRODUCTION

One morning in 415 BC, the citizens of Athens awoke to discover that all the stone Hermae in their streets had been mutilated. Hermae were square stone pillars bearing a phallic image (intended to avert evil), and topped by a bust of Hermes; they were placed outside the doors of houses and temples, at crossroads, and as boundary markers or signposts. They were viewed with such reverence that to mistreat them verged on blasphemy, and could only be an ill omen – one of especial menace given that the Athenians, engaged in the Peloponnesian War, were about to launch their fleet against Sicily. In the ensuing atmosphere of panic, denunciations flowed in. Although nobody knew who had mutilated the Hermae, other sacred images had previously been damaged by some young men on a drunken spree, who had compounded their crime by holding a mock celebration of the Eleusinian Mysteries at home. One of them was Alcibiades, a brilliant, erratic, dazzlingly handsome figure who was a close companion of Socrates, himself suspected of idiosyncratic religious beliefs. (It is Alcibiades who, rather the worse for wear, bursts in on the drinking party recorded or invented by Plato in the *Symposium*, where he proceeds to launch into a tipsy but eloquent panegyric of Socrates.) Alcibiades had already been appointed one of the three leaders of the Sicilian expedition. He offered to stand trial on the charges now brought against him, but was allowed to accompany the expedition for the time being. When recalled, soon afterwards, from Sicily to face his accusers (he had in fact been sentenced to death *in absentia*), he instead defected to Sparta. After changing sides several times in the course of the war, he was eventually assassinated in 404.

Let's fast-forward two millennia. One morning in 1530, the citizens of Rome awoke to discover that some of the bas-reliefs on the Arch of Constantine, and the statues of Apollo and the Muses in the portico of the ancient basilica of San Paolo, had been vandalised. This time there was much less doubt about the identity of the perpetrator: Lorenzino de' Medici, with a gang of drunken friends, had carried out these acts of defacement. The Pope, Clement VII, also a Medici, was so angered that he threatened to have Lorenzino hanged, but he was dissuaded by other family members. In any case, the vandal fled to Florence.

Why did Lorenzino commit this act of iconoclasm? Nobody knows. Some say it was jealousy of his cousin, Cardinal Ippolito (yet another Medici), who was forever enriching his collections of ancient statues from pagan Rome. Some say it was a more general act of adolescent and vaguely Oedipal rebellion. And some say that it was part of the 'antic disposition' that the young Lorenzino had already started to affect. 'Antic' means both 'madcap' and 'antique'. Maybe Lorenzino's eccentricity was his way of emulating an ancient model, Alcibiades, equally brilliant and well connected, but equally unbalanced and unpredictable. Lorenzino was playing a part that in some sense had been scripted for him – by Thucydides or Plutarch, perhaps, both of whom had given accounts of Alcibiades' dangerous allure and eccentric behaviour.

The ruler of the Florence where Lorenzino took refuge was also a Medici, of course: Alessandro de' Medici. He had been imposed on Florence after one of its last outbursts of republican feeling, in which the Medici had been ousted in 1527. The armies of both Pope and Emperor (Clement VII and Charles V respectively) thereupon subjected the city to an

eleven-month siege; it capitulated on 12th August 1530. The next year, with imperial and papal support, Alessandro was installed as 'head of the government and of the state', soon (in 1532) to have this title upgraded to 'hereditary Duke' and 'perpetual gonfalonier' of the Florentine Republic – though not much in the way of republican institutions was left: Alessandro was the *de facto* tyrant. A certain rough charm won a grudging affection from his subjects, before the downsides of his character became evident: he was a lecher who preyed on the daughters and wives of his citizens, he was vicious and unscrupulous in the pursuit of absolute power, he enriched himself through extortionate taxes, he had opponents murdered or driven out of Florence. Lorenzino proceeded to become his sidekick: his companion in drinking and debauchery, his buffoon and the butt of his sarcasm. They were often seen galloping through the streets on the same horse, hurling abuse at bypassers. They frequented brothels and violated convents. They both enjoyed dressing up as women; they may have shared the same bed. There is an interesting sidelight on this period of Lorenzino's life in the memoirs of the goldsmith and sculptor Benvenuto Cellini, who was commissioned by Alessandro to make a medallion of him. Typically, on one occasion when Cellini turned up to show the wax model of this medallion, he found the Duke in bed, and was told he had just been engaged in debauchery. Present at the interview was Lorenzino. Cellini told the Duke that he would make a much finer medal of him than he had done of Pope Clement VII, and then added that Lorenzino would no doubt provide some beautiful design for the medal's reverse side – to which Lorenzino immediately assented, adding that he would like to do something that would amaze the whole world. Again we encounter the theme of statues (or medals: the aesthetic

transfiguration of power) and their reverse (or underside, or potential defacement).

Nobody knows how much of Lorenzino's complicity with Alessandro's vices was real, and how much was feigned, part of a long-term tactic to gain the confidence and intimacy of the tyrant so that he could eventually slay him. Having emulated Alcibiades, Lorenzino, in his antic disposition, verging on real madness, may have anticipated Hamlet, another melancholy jester with a hidden agenda: to kill a 'tyrant', a 'usurper', who is and is not a kinsman (just as Alessandro, with his ambiguous parentage, may or may not have been a distant cousin of Lorenzino). Despite, or because of, this apparent lunacy, Alessandro himself, who seems to have been strangely attracted to his enigmatic companion, called Lorenzino 'the philosopher'. The Florentines called him, more bluntly, 'Lorenzaccio' – 'nasty Lorenzo'. (*Lorenzaccio* is the name of the 1834 closet drama by Alfred de Musset which exploits the similarities between Lorenzino and Hamlet, and forcefully brings out the extent to which Lorenzino's mask of vice sticks. Having become just as debauched and corrupt as the Duke, he can salvage his earlier republican idealism only by an act of murder that will inevitably lead to his own death.)

Lorenzino's plans crystallised at the beginning of 1537. His aunt Caterina Soderini Ginori was a conspicuously virtuous wife and thus an ideally challenging target for Alessandro's powers of seduction. Taking advantage of the Epiphany holidays, Lorenzino would bring Caterina to his, Lorenzino's house, on Saturday evening (5th January 1537). Here Alessandro would be waiting. Alessandro, in a state of undress and with his sword unbuckled, was lying in a state of somnolent expectation when into his room came Lorenzino and a hired assassin, Scoronconcolo. 'Are you asleep?' Lorenzino

asked Alessandro, and then thrust his sword into the Duke's stomach. The ensuing brawl was prolonged. Alessandro put up fierce resistance, biting Lorenzino's thumb to the bone; Scoronconcolo plunged his dagger into the Duke's throat. Once they were sure Alessandro was dead, Lorenzino fled to Bologna, his bleeding hand covered by a glove.

What should he have done at this juncture? In his *Apology* he deals with those of his critics who thought he should have mimicked not Alcibiades, but another character from antiquity, the republican 'tyrannicide' Brutus, and taken a stand. Maybe he should have followed the promptings of Cassius in *Julius Caesar*, who urges his fellow conspirators, bearing daggers red with Caesar's blood, to go 'to the common pulpits, and cry out "Liberty, freedom, and enfranchisement!"' – or, as Lorenzino himself sourly remarks, perhaps he was supposed to chop off Alessandro's head and carry it through the streets of Florence in an attempt to rouse the Florentines to throw off the yoke of servitude.

In fact, Lorenzino did none of these things. He merely ensured, before leaving the scene of the crime, that he locked the door and took the key with him. It was only when Alessandro's bodyguard complained about having to stand around outside Lorenzino's house that Cardinal Cybo, late on Sunday evening, had the room broken into and Alessandro's body was revealed. Perhaps Lorenzino thought he had done his bit and it was now for the Florentines, assisted by the anti-Medician exiles outside the city, to take up the cause. To some extent they did so. Cellini records that, on the night Alessandro was murdered, he saw a strange light over Florence and, as yet unaware of the events, deduced that it was some portent. Back in Rome, the news of the Duke's death soon arrived, and Francesco Soderini sneeringly told the

artist that this act was indeed the reverse of the tyrant's medal that Lorenzino had promised, and that whereas Cellini had been happy to immortalise Alessandro in art, 'we want no more Dukes!' Cellini retorted that, before very long, Florence would simply have another Duke. He was right. After some deliberation, the city's leaders decided to nominate Cosimo de' Medici as Alessandro's successor. He routed an army of exiles at Montemurlo, near Prato, in August 1537 – a battle which, according to the disdainful report in Lorenzino's *Apology*, the rebels, under the leadership of Piero Strozzi, threw away. While Piero escaped, many others were captured. Cosimo had sixteen of their leaders executed in the Piazza della Signoria in batches of four, on four successive mornings. Cosimo himself was eventually given papal approval for his sovereign status, and was crowned Grand Duke of Tuscany by Pius V in 1570.

Lorenzino, meanwhile, began his wanderings, aware that his life was in danger from the agents of Cosimo. During the decade following the death of Alessandro, he wrote his *Apology*, justly celebrated as a fine and poignant piece of Renaissance rhetoric. It is a compelling work, calling on classical *exempla* (Alessandro is seen as worse than tyrants such as Nero, Caligula and Phalaris; Lorenzino, it is implied, is as noble as the great and disinterested tyrannicides such as Brutus), bitterly berating the Florentines who had failed to follow *his* example of republican fervour, and claiming that his act had been impelled by nothing other than civic virtue.

It contrasts with the account of Francesco Bibboni (alias Cecchino da Bibbona), the killer acting on Cosimo's orders, who eventually tracked Lorenzino down to Venice and murdered him in 1548, for money. Two murders and two 'apologias' for murder: how are we to judge between them?

It is tempting (chiasmus is always tempting) to say that Lorenzino was just as much a mercenary thug as Bibboni, or that Bibboni at least had the honesty to portray himself as a professional assassin doing a 'job' ('*negozio*'). We can speculate that Lorenzino was impelled by a desire for fame, or jealousy of the Duke's power, or that the murder was the result of a complex love-hate emotion he felt for Alessandro (Musset has *his* Lorenzaccio claiming to have kissed the remnants of Alessandro's orgies on his lips). The lofty republican sentiments of the *Apology* would then merely conceal this tangled knot of motives, whereas Bibboni – who at least never pretended to cosy up to his victim in the way Lorenzino did to Alessandro – was your plain and honest bruiser. (For this reason, taking my cue from the vernacular style of his report, I have not scrupled to foist on him a caricatural version of the language of a modern-day hitman, an archetypal dodgy geezer.)

Bibboni seems to have made his peace with the world: no doubt he died, when he did (in Volterra, in 1595, aged nearly eighty) in the bosom of the Church. Lorenzino, who protests fiercely against the charge that he should not have killed someone who trusted him, has to struggle against the enormous weight of condemnation associated with treachery in the minds of Italians familiar with Dante's *Inferno*. In that semi-Christianised but at times stubbornly pagan work, Dante reserves the deepest depths of Hell for traitors to their lords – Judas first and foremost, but with the tyrannicides Brutus and Cassius to keep him company. One can sense where Dante, who in the *Inferno* is himself something of a cultural tyrant, with fierce and unpredictable passions and dark irrational prejudices, might have consigned Lorenzino. And for Lorenzino to identify himself with Brutus was to act

in defiance of this powerful indictment of tyrannicide as damnable.

Our age is iconoclastic: it loves defacing sacred monuments and mutilating the Hermae of culture. But what if its suspicions, in Lorenzino's case, are ill-founded? True, we must look behind the façade of Lorenzino's self-justifying pleas and question the nobility of his motives (did he want power for himself? – though admittedly his actions, in that case, seem somewhat counter-intuitive). We need, as it were, to see through his attempt to strike a medal of liberty with his own countenance embossed on its obverse side. And we need to bear in mind how, here as often, tyrannicide fails to undermine the deeply entrenched structures of power: the death of one 'tyrant' (Julius Caesar, Alessandro) leads to the installation of another (Augustus, Cosimo). Modernity is also more aware of the way that internalised tyrants can be as powerful as real political tyrants, and more difficult to get rid of. 'But in here it is I must kill the priest and the king,' says Stephen Dedalus in *Ulysses*, tapping his brow. Lorenzino's act was a blow for freedom in the most ambiguous sense. But there is no reason to deprive him of the purity of his intentions. Alessandro was not Hitler, but the peroration of Lorenzino's *Apology* uses similar language to that of people implicated in plots to remove Hitler – Count Yorck von Wartenburg, for instance, executed on 8th June 1944, whose last letters, to his mother and wife, claim: 'My actions were in no way motivated by ambitious thoughts or desires for power. My actions have been determined purely by my patriotic feeling, by concern for my Germany… I too am dying for my fatherland.' True, the question inevitably forces itself on us: where *is* our *Vaterland* or *patria*? But what is not in doubt is that, wherever it may be, it cannot be a tyranny, and that if it is, to assent to the status

quo is wicked, while to rid oneself of that tyranny, especially by violence, is to run moral risks of the utmost gravity.

In 1504, ten years before the birth of Lorenzino, who in his youth would have passed it countless times, Michelangelo's statue of David was placed outside the Palazzo Vecchio in Florence. Much media attention has focused, in recent months, on how (or indeed whether) it ought to be cleaned – as it is being cleaned – for its five-hundredth anniversary. Rather less attention has been paid to what the statue might have meant for Michelangelo's fellow-Florentines – David as a freedom-fighter, struggling against superior odds: a tyrannicide, in so far as every tyrant is a Goliath. When Lorenzino asks his compatriots whether he was supposed to cut off Alessandro's head as a sign of liberty, the image of the young, vulnerable David may well have been haunting his imagination: a David whose giant-killing was in its way a providential act of emancipation. The *Apology* can stand as a similar statue, easy enough to deface but thought-provoking nonetheless, of Lorenzino-Lorenzaccio, the melancholy court jester and defender, in his own troubled and enigmatic way, of civic virtue.

Note on the Text:

My translation is based on the edition of Lorenzino's *Apologia* and Francesco Bibboni's *Morte di Lorenzino de' Medici* published by L'Istituto Editoriale Italiano in its 'Biblioteca di Classici' series (*L'Apologia e l'Aridosio*, ed. by Massimo Bontempelli, Milan: IEI, 1916). The other sources I have consulted include the *Storia Fiorentina* by Benedetto Varchi (the principal origin for Musset's *Lorenzaccio*, and another version of the story by George Sand); L. A. Ferrai's *Lorenzino de' Medici e la società cortigiana del Cinquecento* (Milan:

Apology for a Murder

If I had to justify my actions to those who do not know what liberty is, nor tyranny either, I would endeavour to demonstrate and to prove with reasons – of which there are many – that men ought not to desire anything more than they desire civic life, that is, a life lived in liberty, since good civic order is rarer and less enduring in any other regime than it is in a republic. I would also demonstrate that, since tyranny is totally contrary to civic life, they should therefore hate it above all things; and since this opinion has so frequently prevailed in the past, those who have liberated their fatherland from tyranny have been considered almost as worthy of suitable honours as have those who established their fatherland in the first place. But since the reader I wish to address is one who knows, both in theory and in practice, that liberty is good, and tyranny bad, I can take it for granted that this is a universal truth, and so I will speak of my own action in particular, not craving any reward or praise for it, but in order to demonstrate that not only did I perform a deed incumbent on any good citizen, but that I would have failed in my duty to my fatherland and to myself if I had not performed it.

And so, to begin with the most well-known facts, I will recall that there is no one who does not doubt that Duke Alessandro (so-called de' Medici) was a tyrant of our fatherland, apart from those who, by flattering him and supporting his party, grew rich; and even these could not be so ignorant, or so blinded by their own interests, as to fail to recognise that he was indeed a tyrant. But since they themselves gained greatly from his power, and cared little for the public good, they threw in their lot with his fortunes. They were, truth to tell, men of little quality, and few in number, and so cannot in any way outweigh the judgement of the rest of the world, which considered him to be a tyrant – nor can they outweigh

the truth. The city of Florence, after all, has from ancient times been the possession of its people; it thus ensues that all those who rule it without being elected by the people to do so are tyrants, as was the case with the Medici family, which gained control of our city for many years with the consent and participation of a minority of the people. But for all this, they never had more than a limited authority until, after many vicissitudes and changes in regime, Pope Clement came, with that violence known to everyone, and deprived his own fatherland of liberty, making that same Alessandro its master.[1]

Alessandro, on arrival in Florence, took steps to ensure there could be no doubt that he was indeed a tyrant, by sweeping away all public virtue, and every relic of republican life, even the very name of 'republic'; and, as if it were a necessary condition for any tyrant to be no less evil than Nero, no less a hater of mankind and lecherous than Caligula, and no less cruel than Phalaris[2], sought to surpass all of them in wickedness. For, over and above the cruelties he inflicted on the citizens, which were no less appalling than those inflicted by the former tyrants, he surpassed Nero's wickedness in killing his mother – Nero, after all, committed the deed since he feared he might otherwise lose his power and his life, and thus acted so as to forestall the plot he feared was being hatched against himself; but Alessandro committed that infamy out of mere cruelty and inhumanity, as I will shortly relate. And he was in no way inferior to Caligula in the contempt, ridicule and torment with which he oppressed the citizens, with his adulteries and his acts of violence, his coarse, harsh words and his menaces, which are, to men who esteem honour, harder to bear than death – which he eventually inflicted on them. He greatly outdid Phalaris in cruelty, since, whilst Phalaris punished Perillus quite justly for the cruel device the latter had

invented, designed to inflict agonising torture and death on his victims in the bronze bull, it is easy to imagine that Alessandro would have actually rewarded the inventor, if he had lived in his time.[3] He himself was always dreaming up new kinds of torture and death, such as walling up men alive in such confined spaces that they could not bend or turn or change position, but were, so to speak, as much imprisoned in the wall as the bricks and stones; and in this state he kept them alive, feeding them the bare minimum and prolonging their agony to an impossible degree, since the mere death of his citizens was not enough to sate this monster. So the seven years that he spent as ruler can be compared, for lust, avarice, cruelty, and wickedness with any seven years of Nero, Caligula or Phalaris, even if one were to choose the most wicked years of their whole lives – bearing in mind the proportionate size of the cities and realms involved. For even in this brief time, so many citizens were driven out of their fatherland, great numbers of them subsequently being persecuted and killed in exile; so many were beheaded without trial and without cause, merely on the pretext of empty fears and words of no importance; and others were poisoned or killed by his own hands or by his accomplices, simply so that he need not feel ashamed in front of certain men who had witnessed the conditions of his birth and upbringing. Furthermore, deeds of extortion and rapine and acts of adultery were so rife, and such widespread violence was committed against things both secular and sacred, that it will seem difficult to decide whether the tyrant is more blameworthy for his evil and wickedness, or the people of Florence for being meek and cowardly and putting up with such dire calamities for so many years – as it was, at the time, much more dangerous to accept the status quo than to embark, with some hope of success, on the

task of liberating the fatherland and making their lives safe for the future.

Therefore, any who might think that Alessandro should not be called a tyrant since he was given power over Florence by the Emperor – who is deemed to have the authority to appoint whatever men he sees fit to rule over any state – are wrong. For even if the Emperor does have such authority, he does not have the authority to act in this way without just cause, and as far as Florence in particular is concerned, he had absolutely no right to do so, since in the agreement he drew up with the Florentine people at the end of the siege of 1530[4], it was expressly declared that he could not place that city under the dominion of the Medici family. And quite apart from that, even if the Emperor had indeed had the authority to act in this way, and had done so with every reason and justification in the world, so that Alessandro's legitimacy as ruler had been greater than that of the King of France, his dissolute life, his avarice and his cruelty would have made of him a tyrant. This is evident if we consider the example of Hieron and Hieronymos of Syracuse[5]: one of them was called 'king' and the other 'tyrant', the reason being that Hieron led such a holy life, as the writers relate, that he was loved as long as he lived, and his citizens missed him when he was dead; but his son Hieronymos, who might have seemed more securely ensconced in power, and more legitimately established by rights of succession, was throughout his villainous life so hated by those same citizens that he lived and died as a tyrant; and those who assassinated him were praised and celebrated, whereas, if they had killed his father, they would have been censured and held to be parricides. The lesson is this: it is their way of life that leads rulers to become tyrants, in spite of all the investitures, all the justifications and all the rights of succession in the world.

But so as not to waste any more words proving something that is clearer than the noonday sun, let me now turn to those who claim that, even if he were indeed a tyrant, I should not have assassinated him, since I was a servant of his, a member of his family, and a man he trusted. I would not wish to see such men punished for their envy and ill-will in any other way than by God making them kinsmen, servants and confidants of the tyrant of their fatherland – if it is not too wicked to wish so much suffering on a city for the fault of a few. They try to blacken my good intentions with these calumnies, but even if the latter were true, they would not be strong enough to prevail, especially since I maintain that I never was a servant of Alessandro, nor he a member of my family or any kinsman of mine; and I will prove that he never willingly took me into his trust. There are two senses in which a man may be said to be a bondsman or servant of another: either because he is rewarded for serving him and staying loyal to him; or because he is his slave, since subjects are not usually included in this category of bondsman and servant. That I was not Alessandro's slave is perfectly obvious, just as it is equally obvious (to anyone who takes the trouble to think about it) that I not only received no reward or wages from him, but paid him my portion of taxes, as did the other citizens; and if he believed that I was his subject or vassal, since he had more power than I did, he should have realised that he was mistaken, once we were on an equal footing; as a result, I never was, nor could ever be called, his servant. That he was not a member of the Medici family or any kinsman of mine is evident, since he was born to a woman of the lowest and basest class, from Collevecchio, near Rome, who was a housemaid of Duke Lorenzo, performing the humblest household tasks, and was married to a coach driver.[6] So far, all this is absolutely

clear. It may be doubted whether Duke Lorenzo, who was exiled at the time, had anything to do with this woman; and if it did happen, it happened no more than once; but who is so ignorant of the consensus of mankind and its laws as not to know that, when a woman has a husband and he lives in the same place as she does, even if she is immoral and flaunts her body in front of every man's lust, all the children she produces are always adjudged to be, and are in fact, her husband's, since the laws wish to preserve decency as much as possible? And so, if this servant woman from Collevecchio (and, as regards her titles of nobility, nobody even knows either her first name or her surname) was married to a coach driver, as is clearly known to everyone, Alessandro, in accordance with human and divine laws, was the son of that coach driver and not of Duke Lorenzo. In consequence, he had no more in common with me than the mere fact that he was the son of a coach driver who happened to work for the Medici family. That he did not trust me I can easily prove: he would never consent to allow me to carry weapons, but always kept me unarmed, as he did the other citizens, all of whom he feared and suspected. What is more, he never trusted himself to be alone with me, even though I never bore weapons and he was always armed, but he always had three or four of his accomplices with him; nor would he have risked being with me on that night which was to prove his last, had it not been for his unbridled lust, which so blinded him that it made him change his habits, quite contrary to his intentions. But how could he have ever trusted me, when he never trusted any man in the world? And he never did love anyone, and usually men cannot trust anyone else except those whom they love. And that he never loved anyone, but indeed hated everyone, can be seen from the fact that he hated and harried – contriving to bring about their

deaths by poison – the people closest to him, the very ones who should have been dearest: his mother, and Cardinal Ippolito de' Medici, who was thought to be his cousin.[7] I would not like the enormity of his wicked deeds to make you think that I have made all this up so as to add weight to my accusations. I am so far from having made it up that I am stating the case as plainly as I can, so as not to make his crimes seem more incredible than they are by their very nature. But there are innumerable witnesses, countless detailed reports and recent accounts that speak loud and clear, and all lead to the firm conclusion that this monster, this prodigy of crime, had his own mother poisoned, for no other reason than that, as long as she remained alive, he considered her as evidence of his own low birth. Indeed, although he had been politically prominent for many years, he had left her in her poverty, consigned to ordinary activities in the household or out in the fields, so that those citizens who had fled from our city to escape the tyrant's cruelty and avarice, together with those who had been driven out by him, decided to take his mother with them to the Emperor in Naples, to show His Majesty from what low birth the man he was allowing to rule Florence had sprung.[8] Thus Alessandro, not merely because he was ashamed of his mother and so ignored the filial piety and love due to her (a love that in any case he never felt), but out of his innate cruelty and savagery, ensured that she was killed before she could be brought into Caesar's presence. How very difficult this must have been for him one can judge by imagining what a poor old woman she was, spinning wool and feeding the sheep. Even if she no longer hoped for any kindliness from her son, at least she had not anticipated such an inhuman and horrendous deed; and had he not been, as well as the cruellest, the most foolish man in the world, he

could have taken her to some other place in secret, where even if he had been unwilling to treat her as his mother, he could at least have kept her alive, rather than being prepared to add such disgraceful and unspeakable wickedness to his list of ignominious crimes.

So, returning to my main point, I conclude that, since he loved neither his mother, nor Cardinal Ippolito de' Medici, nor anyone else from among his closest kin, he never loved anyone at all, and in consequence never trusted anyone either – since, as I have already said, we cannot trust those we do not love; and I was therefore never his servant, nor his kinsman, nor did he ever trust me. But it seems clear to me that those who, being badly informed or for some other reason, say that I was wrong to assassinate Alessandro, and support their claim by appealing to the aforementioned reasons, show themselves to be woefully ignorant of the laws ordained against tyrants, and the actions that are commonly praised by humankind, since men have at times slain even their own brothers for the liberty of their fatherland. Moreover, if the laws not only permit but constrain the son to denounce his father, should the latter attempt to make himself tyrant over his fatherland, was not I all the more obliged to try to liberate my already enslaved fatherland by the death of one man, who, even if he had been a member of my family (which he was not), in their view, was still a bastard, and five or six degrees removed from me in kinship? And if Timoleon found himself forced to kill his own brother to liberate his fatherland, and was so praised and celebrated for his deed – as indeed he still is – how can those malevolent men assume they have the authority to censure me? But as far as killing someone who trusts you (which I am not saying I did), I insist that, even if I had done as much, I would not have been wrong; and if I could not have

acted otherwise, I would still have done it. I put it to these men: if their fatherland were oppressed by a tyrant, would they first invite him to fight in his own defence, informing him that they wished to kill him, knowing that they were thus risking their own deaths – or would they not rather try to kill him by whatever means they could, using all the tricks and stratagems at their disposal to ensure that he stay dead and they stay alive? For my part, I think that they would not take the trouble to kill him either way; there is no other conclusion to be drawn, since they censure the man who has taken the most obvious route. If this consensus, indeed this law, that is held as sacrosanct among men – that we should not deceive those who trust us – were abolished, I am fully convinced that it would be better to be a beast than a man, since men would then be deprived, essentially, of trust, friendship, harmony and most of the other qualities that make us superior to the brute beasts, since in every other respect many of them are stronger than we are, and have more vitality, and are less subject to the chances and necessities of human life. But this does not justify drawing the conclusion that this trust and this friendship should be maintained even with tyrants, since, just as they pervert and confound all laws and good customs, so likewise are men obliged, against all laws and all established usage, to try to rid the earth of them; and the sooner they do so, the more praiseworthy they are. To be sure, it would be a good law for tyrants, this law that you would like to introduce – but it would be a bad law for everyone else, if no one were supposed to harm a tyrant who trusted them. After all, if he trusts everyone, according to your law he could not be harmed by anyone, and he would not need guards or fortresses.[9] Thus I conclude that tyrants, in whatever way they are assassinated, should be slain.

Now I turn to those who say that I was wrong, not so much in killing Alessandro, but in the way I behaved after his death. It will be a little more difficult to reply to these than it was to the others, since the way things turned out seems to justify their opinion. They are completely swayed by the turn of events, without taking anything else into account, though wise men are so far from judging things from their effects alone that they tend to praise good and wise deeds even if they produce bad results, and censure bad deeds even if they produce good results. I want, furthermore, to demonstrate that I could not have done any more than I did; indeed, had I attempted more, it would have led to my cause being harmed and myself censured. Let me say, then, that my aim was to liberate Florence; and killing Alessandro was the means to this end. But since I knew that this was an endeavour which I could not carry out alone, and I did not want to share it with anyone because of the obvious risk inherent in broadcasting such plans – a risk not so much to one's life, but to one's ability to see the job through to a successful conclusion – I resolved to perform my task without any company, in so far as this was possible, and to bring in someone else to help me only when I could no longer manage by myself. This plan worked up to the death of Alessandro, since until that time I had been self-sufficient; but from then on, I started to need outside help, since I found myself alone, without friends and confidants, and I had no weapons other than the sword with which I had slain him.

Since I found it necessary to request aid, I could expect to place my hopes more profitably in those outside Florence than those inside the city; because I had seen with what ardour and spirit the former were seeking to regain their liberty, and, conversely, with what meekness and cowardice those in Florence were bearing their servitude. I knew that a number of

those who had in 1530 gathered to defend their liberty with such manly virtue were still there, and that the rest had sought voluntary exile; hence I could place greater hope in the exiles than in those who had remained in the city, since the latter were living under tyranny, whereas the former were prepared to be rebels rather than slaves. I also knew that the exiles were armed, and those within the city entirely unarmed; furthermore, I considered it certain that the exiles were unanimous in their desire for liberty, while I knew that in Florence there was also an admixture of men who were happy to live under tyranny. It later became evident that events bore out the correctness of this judgement, since in the entire city, at this crucial juncture, there was nobody who bore himself, I will not say as a good citizen, but even just as a man, with the exception of two or three. And those who censure me seem to want me to have gone through the city summoning the people to liberty, and showing them their tyrant dead; and they want my words to have moved the people to action, when as they know the people were not moved by deeds. So should I have shouldered that dead body like a porter, and gone shouting through Florence like a madman? I will merely say that Piero, my servant, who had behaved with such spirit in helping me to commit the murder, was so overcome by cowardice once the deed was done, and once he had had time to reflect on the risk he had run and was still running, that I could make no further use of him. And did I not have to fear that, being surrounded by the tyrant's guards, and so to speak in the very same house where all his servants lived – especially since the night happened to be lit up by the most dazzling moonlight – I might well be attacked and killed before I had taken three steps outside the door? And if I had cut off his head, and managed to conceal it under a mantle, where was I supposed to have

made for, being alone, and knowing nobody in Florence whom I could trust to believe me? After all, a decapitated head is such a disfigured thing that, if you also take into account the usual fear people have of being led astray or deceived (especially by me, whom they considered to hold exactly the opposite political opinion to the one I really had), I could expect to find someone who would kill me rather than someone who would believe me. And my death was no small matter in these circumstances, since it would have lent credence to the enemy party, and those who desired tyranny, since it might seem that with my murder, Alessandro's death would have been partly avenged; and if I were to follow such a course, I might harm my cause rather than further it. So I took quite the opposite view to those men and, rather than making public the death of Alessandro, I sought to conceal it as much as I could at the time, and I carried off with me the key to the room where I had left him dead. I would, after all, have wished, if the thing had been possible, that the discovery of the tyrant's death might be delayed until the news had arrived that the exiles were on their way home to win back liberty. It was not my fault that this did not happen.

Others say that I ought to have called the tyrant's guard, and showed him to them, dead, and asked them to protect me and hail me there and then as his successor – in short, to entrust myself to their mercies. Then, once I had gained power, I would have restored the republic, as was right and proper. Those who look at it this way at least acknowledge that absolutely no trust could be placed in the people; but they do not realise that if those soldiers, grief-stricken at seeing their lord lying there dead, had in the heat of the moment killed me, as they most probably would have done, then I would have lost at once life and honour, since everyone

would have believed that I had wanted to make myself a tyrant, and not to liberate the fatherland. As nothing has ever been further from my own mind, I have endeavoured to keep such an idea equally far from the minds of others.

So in the one case I would have harmed my cause, and in the other, my honour. But I would readily confess to having made a mistake in not choosing one of these or similar paths, if I had not had some cause to hope that the exiles would feel obliged to help me finish the task I had begun. After all, I had seen them recently coming to Naples, all men of repute and determination, and all unanimous in their repeated demands for liberty in the presence of the tyrant, who was not only alive, but was also the son-in-law of the very Emperor from whom they were requesting that liberty – so was I not justified in judging that, since the tyrant was now dead, and the Emperor was in Spain and not in Naples, they would certainly redouble the strength and the determination I had seen in them, and return to win back liberty for themselves? To be sure, I would have thought it mean of myself not to have placed such hopes in them, and too trusting in them if I had not taken the first steps myself. I confess that it never entered my head that Cosimo de' Medici would succeed Alessandro[10]; but even if the thought had occurred to me as a possibility, I would not have behaved in any other way after the death of the tyrant, as I would never have imagined that men whom we esteem as wise could prefer, above true, present and certain glory, uncertain fortune and vile ambition. There is as much difference between talking about things and doing them as there is between actually doing them and then talking about them once the deed is done; so those who now talk so glibly about what I should have done then would, if they had found themselves faced with having to do the deed, have taken more

time to consider how impossible it was to raise to revolt a people demoralised and cowed, beaten, disarmed and divided, with guards to keep them in bodily submission and a fortress[11] to intimidate their minds – a people likely to be all the more terrified as this was a new and unprecedented event in Florence. And it was especially difficult for me since, apart from bearing the Medici name, I was considered to be a supporter of the tyranny. And so, those who talk about things after the fact, and see that they have turned out badly, should try to imagine what advice they would have given me at the time. *Then* they will see how difficult it would have been for me to act alone, while on the other hand there were the exiles, men of such high repute, and as numerous, rich and united in their eagerness for liberty as everyone believed, with nothing to prevent them from returning to Florence now that the tyrant had been done away with. So I believe they would have been of quite the opposite opinion to the one they now hold. In short, it comes down to this: they wanted me, alone and unarmed, to go around rousing and summoning the people to liberty, and setting myself up against those who thought otherwise, which was impossible – whereas I wanted to carry all this out in the company of the exiles, and with the support of the men in positions of authority, the majority of whom I knew supported us; and if we had returned to Florence with the rapidity and resolve that the situation required, we would have encountered no obstacles; not even the election of Cosimo, which was of such dubious legitimacy and so recent, could have impeded or harmed us. And so, if I had found the exiles to be as bold and swift as they should have been – which was the case with the majority of them, although unfortunately they were the less powerful party – even if they had no other quality than being an exile, nobody will deny that my plan

would have turned out just as I had imagined. This can be proved on many grounds that I will omit so as to keep my account short, and can be seen, for example, by the Battle of Montemurlo, which ensued many months after they ought to have taken action, and during which they had allowed their adversaries not only to build up their forces, but also to win the good name that they themselves had lost. They would certainly have succeeded in liberating Florence, if the malevolence and the inept ambition of a few had not given the victory to their adversaries, who had not even dared to hope for it.[12] Though the latter could see with their own eyes that they were the victors, they still could not believe they had actually won, since the exiles had lost a battle that everyone had thought they could not possibly lose. So whoever again refuses to judge events with the benefit of hindsight must acknowledge that they would at that time have liberated Florence, if they had been disciplined; and this would have been all the more certain if, after the death of Alessandro, they had immediately put even half as much effort into it as they did then – which they did not do because they did not want to; no other reason can be put forward.

However, I am prepared to confess to these critics that my own conduct after the death of Alessandro was misguided, if in turn they will confess to me that they reached this conclusion the minute they heard that I had killed him, and was myself safe and sound. But if they came to the opposite conclusion, and deemed that I had done more than enough in killing him and saving myself, and if they immediately decided that, since so many powerful citizens of such high repute were among the exiles, Florence would have her liberty back, I refuse to concede that they can find fault with me, or that they are justified in thinking that I left Florence out of an excessive

desire to save my own skin. They would deem me to be lacking in judgement, if they thought that it had taken me that long to discover that the affair I had embarked on was filled with danger; but if they will consider the matter in its entirety, they will acknowledge that I never thought of my own safety more than was reasonable, and if I then went to Constantinople, I did so when I saw that things had not only turned out badly but were in desperate straits; and if ill-fortune had not persecuted me so bitterly, perhaps that journey would not have been in vain.[13]

For all these reasons I am more justified in boasting that I liberated Florence, having left her free of tyrants, than they are in claiming that I to any degree failed; not only did I slay the tyrant, but I myself went out to exhort and stir up those whom I knew to be both willing and able to do more than others for the liberty of their fatherland. And so, what fault is mine, if I did not find them as eager and as ardent as they should have been? And what more can I do? Just look at what I managed to do without any outside help; did I fail in this? And for the rest, do not ask of men more than they are capable of, and take it as read that (if all the citizens of Florence had been as zealous for their fatherland as they should have been), having had no scruple to openly imperil my life, abandon my mother, my brother and all that was most dear to me, and cause the present ruin of my family to get rid of the tyrant (which was the sole means of seeing my purpose through), to this end, I also would not have hesitated to shed my own blood, and that of those closest to me as well; being fully assured that neither they nor I could have contrived to end our lives more gloriously than in the service of our fatherland.

NOTES

1. Pope Clement VII (1478–1534) had been born in Florence in 1478 as Giulio de' Medici, the illegitimate son of Giuliano de' Medici (1453–78), and was raised by Lorenzo the Magnificent (1449–92). He was Pope from 1523 to 1534. An indecisive character, he sometimes supported Francis I of France (1494–1547) and sometimes the Holy Roman Emperor Charles V (1500–58), with whose support he ensured that Alessandro de' Medici (1510–37) became head of state in 1531.

2. Phalaris, tyrant of Acragas in Sicily (6th century BC), was famous for his cruelty.

3. Perillus invented the bronze bull for his master Phalaris, who shut up his victims in it and roasted them alive. Their roars of pain sounded like those of a real bull. Phalaris, with a fine sense of irony, immediately tried out the contraption on its inventor, who was thus also its first victim.

4. Charles V had besieged Florence for eleven months; the city surrendered in August 1530.

5. Hieron II of Syracuse (d. 216 BC) was a good king and a friend of Rome; on his death his less good grandson Hieronymos (not his son, as Lorenzino claims) broke with Rome and was assassinated shortly afterwards.

6. Alessandro's biological father may have been Lorenzo, Duke of Urbino, or more probably Cardinal Giulio de' Medici – in other words the same man who became Pope Clement VII.

7. Ippolito de' Medici (1511–35) had been installed as a member of the government in Florence by Clement VII, with the aim of his eventually becoming ruler. The Medici, including Ippolito, were driven out in 1527, and Pope Clement decided that Alessandro would make a more effective ruler. Ippolito was made a cardinal and kept away from Florence, but as Alessandro's cruelty raised increasing discontent, several Florentine exiles chose Ippolito as their envoy to Charles V, hoping to persuade the Emperor to remove the tyrant. Ippolito was poisoned (presumably on the orders of Alessandro) on his way to see Charles.

8. Charles V received Alessandro at Naples in 1535 and, despite the complaints of the tyrant's enemies, decided to maintain him in office.

9. Alessandro had built the biggest fortress in Florence, the Fortezza da Basso (now just to the north of the Santa Maria Novella railway station) to keep the populace in subjection.

10. Cosimo de' Medici (1519–74) was elected head of the Florentine Republic in January 1537, straight after the assassination of Alessandro. His election was ratified by Charles V. At first he was to rule with the help of the Florentine senate, assembly and council.

11. The 'fortress' is the one mentioned above (see note 9).

12. Charles V's general defeated a group of anti-Cosimo rebels at the Battle of

Montemurlo on 2nd August 1537. By September of that year Cosimo was calling himself 'Duke', with the approval of Charles V, and any pretence of quasi-republican government was over.

13. After the assassination, Lorenzino went to Bologna, until hearing of the defeat of the exiles at Montemurlo; then to Constantinople in search of military support against the reinstated Duke, then to France, and eventually to Venice.

The Death of
Lorenzino de' Medici

An Account Written in his own Hand
by Captain Francesco Bibboni

I was just back from Germany, where I'd been a soldier in the pay of the Emperor, when who should I meet but Bebo da Volterra in Vicenza. He was staying at Messer Antonio da Roma's, a gent from that town, since he'd made quite a few enemies; and this Messer Antonio was really rather pleased to see me, and asked me to stay with him.

Meanwhile, a certain Messer Francesco Manente, another gent from Vicenza, got himself mixed up in a real nasty spat with certain members of the Guarzi family, and the Luschi family, all of them from Vicenza; they'd been at daggers drawn for several years, with many killings, among both the families of those who'd started the quarrel and the followers of the two parties. So this Messer Francesco asked my friend Messer Antonio where I was living, and would he be prepared to lend him my services for a day. Since he was such a close friend of his, Messer Antonio could hardly refuse. So Bebo and I went with the aforesaid gent to a village called Celsano, where both parties had property, and they all kept men at home ready for action, so that not a day went by without them heading out into open country to settle their differences with cold steel. So there were always men getting killed or wounded.

So, one day, the men in our party made up their minds to attack the opposite party at home, where we killed two of them; and the rest, five of them, shut themselves up in a neighbouring room, and barricaded themselves in. We nabbed all their harquebuses and other weapons, and they had no choice but to abandon the villa and skip off to Vicenza. And it wasn't long before this nasty state of hostilities was replaced by a nice long period of peace and quiet.

Then Bebo took himself off to Padua with the rector of the university, a Milanese chap, and after a while that same rector went off to Milan, taking Bebo with him.

I stayed on in Vicenza with Messer Galeazzo della Seta, since, despite peace breaking out all over, he was still a bit leery; anyway, I was there about ten months, and then I had to go back to Messer Antonio da Roma's. He had seven brothers. They were all pretty chummy with me and suggested I face life's little ups and down with them – on condition that if there was ever any chance of war breaking out, and I fancied a piece of the action, they promised to provide me with twenty-five scudi, weapons, and a horse, and the return fare, so long as I was still in one piece, of course. And if I didn't fancy going, the same deal anyway.

Anyway, like I've said, Bebo was in Milan, and Messer Francesco Vinta of Volterra happened to be there as ambassador of the Duke of Florence[1]. Francesco spotted Bebo there and asked him what he was up to in Milan. He replied that he was a horseman going around seeing a bit of the world.[2]

Then Messer Francesco told him that, seeing as how he'd been away from his own country for so long, he should try and get permission to return, as he could rely on His Excellency's good graces; and he started to play up this attractive prospect, but in such a vague and indirect way that he left old Bebo feeling quite confused. But then he got down to brass tacks, and told him how things were with Lorenzino de' Medici, the nasty little traitor everyone knew about. He, or somebody, ought to try and pay him back for it; and if he, Bebo, would offer to see the job through, Francesco would send him to have a little talk with the Duke. So Bebo said he was up for the job, and Francesco sent him off with a letter to Florence. When Bebo turned up at the Duke's, the latter assured him that he'd restore him to favour in return for him bumping off Lorenzino. On top of this, they say the Duke gave him letters and money for his security. So Bebo took it on, but he also said

he had a mate as was just the man to help him out, and who'd find the job just up his street.

So Bebo came back from Florence to Milan, and then on to Vicenza, where he came to see me and offered me the job.

I said I needed to think it over; in fact, at first I didn't really know which way to turn. But when I twigged that this was what the Duke wanted, I promised to go along, and we teamed up, swearing to each other we'd keep schtum, and not bring anyone else in on the business. So, having shaken on it, we went to Venice to carry out our little plan. And since I knew the whole city of Venice like the back of my hand, and had loads of mates there, it was no great hassle to discover where the aforementioned Lorenzino was hanging out; so we took some lodgings in the same neighbourhood, and morning, noon and night we'd have a little wander round, thinking how to put our plan into action.

But since Lorenzino never set foot out of doors of his palace, we were a bit flummoxed, and pretty stumped as to how we were going to get the job done. But, as the Almighty would have it, Messer Roberto Strozzi[3] came over from France with Captain Cencio Guasconi, and one of his sidekicks called Spagnoletto, i.e. Little Dago, though in fact he came from Navarre, and was a close pal of mine; anyway, as luck would have it, one morning I bumped into Spagnoletto. We were dead chuffed to meet up again, and made a real fuss of each other; and as we were having a chinwag, he told me they were on their way from France to Rome. I told him I wanted to go and pay my humble respects to Messer Roberto, my main man, the boss; and Spagnoletto said this was fine, as Messer Roberto had known me very well in Rome. So the two of us went over to Lorenzino's house (where Roberto Strozzi and Captain Cencio Guasconi had taken rooms), and funnily

enough, Messer Roberto was just going out with Lorenzino. But as there was a whole gang of gents and various other people with them, I couldn't get close to them. Messer Roberto and Lorenzino hopped into a gondola; and as it had been a long time since I'd last seen Lorenzino, and he didn't dress as dapper as he used to, I didn't really recognise him; one minute I thought it was him, and the next I thought maybe it wasn't. I was getting into a state and finally I said to Spagnoletto, 'I think I know that gent over there, but I can't quite remember where I've met him before. Messer Roberto was practically arm in arm with him.'

Spagnoletto told me, 'You know him all right, it's Messer Lorenzino, but don't tell a soul. He's going by the name of Messer Marco, since he's pretty nervous, and there's not many people as know he's taken rooms here in Venice.'

I replied that I was really surprised to see him, and if I could have helped him out a bit, I'd have given my eye teeth to do so. Then I asked him where they were off to just now; he told me they were going to have dinner with Monsignor Giovanni della Casa, the Papal Legate in Venice[4]. Anyway, I didn't leave his side till I'd wormed as much information out of him as I needed.

Spagnoletto had gone off with his bosses for a bit, and then he was given orders to return home; so the two of us went back to the palace where the said Lorenzino was staying, where I was to have dinner with him.

There was one of Lorenzino's stewards, who'd already been with Piero Strozzi in Rome. If Spagnoletto had greeted me like his long-lost brother, Piero gave me an absolutely fantastic welcome, and we palled up together again just like in old times. And before I left, as we were having a bit of a natter, I also found out that Piero Strozzi was paying Lorenzino an

allowance of 1,500 scudi per year, and he'd given him three bruisers, real hard men, for personal security; and he'd also given him a palace that he paid fifty scudi in rent for; but Lorenzino had taken a palace in the San Paolo district that cost him 300 scudi, so that Piero, because of Lorenzino's extravagance, took 1000 scudi off his allowance, with the result that he was left with only 500 scudi per year. It's perfectly true that when Lorenzino thought Strozzi was leaving him in the lurch, as he'd cut down his annual allowance, he kicked up a hell of a stink, and so Strozzi gave him Alessandro Soderini, another rebel, to keep him company. I was pleased as Punch to have got this information: it was pretty crucial for the job I had to do.

I also found out when he was going to return to the new palace; and through this servant of his, an old and close pal of mine – Luca his name was – I got to know everything he did, easy as pie: even how often he used to flob, in a manner of speaking. Then I found out that this same Lorenzino was head over heels in love with the beautiful Barozza[5], and I discovered how he'd been sweet-talking his way into her affections. So I decided it was time to get the job done, as I'll tell you in a minute or two.

On the Shrove Thursday of Carnival, 3rd February 1548, Lorenzino joined in with the maskers and dressed himself up as a gypsy woman, with other people all tarted up in various costumes, all on horseback – they were breaking a lance or two on the square in front of Santo Spirito. We were thinking and thinking how to see the business through, but couldn't figure out how to do it; all the same, as far as I was concerned, I made good and sure that me and that trusty servant kept abreast of everything that his boss did and said every day. I listened to his information and took the necessary steps: that way I felt

sure as sure could be, and without his help we'd never have managed.

Now that I'd got this far, I chummed up with a shoemaker. One day I'd buy one thing from him, and another, another. Soon we were bosom pals, and the reason was that this same shoemaker's workshop looked out over the whole of the San Paolo square, and in particular Lorenzino's palace, where I'd cool my heels from dawn to dusk. This lasted quite a long period of time; I'd often make out I was having forty winks, though in fact I was keeping a pretty sharp eye on things.

Well, one day I was told that Lorenzino had gone to have dinner with Monsignor Giovanni della Casa; on hearing this news, we all went off, cheerfully resolved to get the job done; and I, bold as brass, climbed the steps into Monsignor Giovanni's palace, leaving Bebo downstairs in the loggia, and told him to be prepared for all eventualities. But we found that Monsignor Giovanni and Lorenzino had gone on to have dinner in Murano, so that we were left empty-handed. After that we made sure to take the trouble to get up-to-date information every day. And since Bebo didn't know Lorenzino, I pointed him out one day – this was when Lorenzino had come back to live in the San Paolo square, where, since they were new to the district, they can't have known their way around the local streets very well, as was proved when one morning, going through the streets to pay a visit to his little lady, the beautiful Barozza, they took the wrong turning; and on the way to a friars' convent, where she used to go to mass, they went down a different street, which took them quite a bit out of the way, and eventually led to a dead end. So we followed them, hoping to carry out our little errand, but we couldn't catch up with them, and so we turned right round and came back; and the men who hadn't been able

to get through that street also turned back. As a result, we met them in a spot where the weapons we had with us wouldn't have been right for the job in hand; so we realised we needed to get ourselves kitted with other weapons, more suitable for the occasion. We reckoned that we might bump into them some other time and get involved in a little fracas in the same spot – as did eventually happen.

On 13th March, the second Sunday in Lent, as I'd gone, as usual, to find out whether Lorenzino had made arrangements to go out, like on previous occasions, I popped into the shoe-maker's workshop, the one I mentioned above, and hung around there for a while, until Lorenzino appeared at his window with a big towel round his neck, combing his hair. At the same moment I saw, going in and then coming out again, a half-pint little bloke called Giovan Battista Martelli, who acted as Lorenzino's minder, with his sword at his side. I thought to myself that Lorenzino himself must be planning to go out, so I went home to get ready and pick up the necessary weapons. I found Bebo there, still fast asleep in bed. I told him to shake a leg, and we made our way to the place where we usually kept a lookout, by San Paolo's church, right at the head of the square, where they'd be passing by. This church is situated like it was on an island, and it's got two doors opposite each other; so I stationed Bebo at the door in front of the church, and told him to stand guard there, and keep an eye open on the workshop. The minute he spotted I'd left it, he was to get going, and I'd follow him.

Now, as our luck would have it, the very same Giovan Battista Martelli came out, and walked a short way ahead; then out came Lorenzino, and then Alessandro Soderini, and they followed each other in a straight line, like a flock of cranes; and when Lorenzino came behind the church of San Paolo, he

lifted the reed matting which hung at the church entrance, so that Bebo, who was standing at the other entrance, saw him; and he also saw me, as I'd come out of the workshop, and we met in the middle of the street, as agreed, and he told me he was in the church; and as I stood watching the exit, I saw Lorenzino coming out of the church, and setting off down the main road, followed by Alessandro Soderini; and I followed them. When we reached the place we'd agreed on, I jumped out in front of Alessandro, dagger in hand, saying, 'Cheer up, Alessandro, you can go your way with the Almighty – it's not you we're after!' But he flung himself on me, and grabbed my arms and held me tight, shouting his head off. I saw I'd completely blown it in thinking I could let him get away in one piece, and I wriggled like hell to get out of his grip, but it so happened that I'd got my dagger free, so I lashed out, as God would have it, at his forehead, so that he started bleeding a bit.[6] This narked him, and he gave me such a violent shove that I fell flat on my back: the ground was slippery, as there'd been a bit of a drizzle. Alessandro reached for his sword, which was in his hand with his sheath, and hit out at my mush, and he caught me on the breastplate of my cuirass, and it was a good thing for me that it was double-knitted chain mail.

Before I'd managed to get back on my feet, he lashed out at me again – three hits he scored, or three thrusts, to be more precise; and if I'd had just ordinary chain mail on my cuirass, he'd have run me through for certain, as I was still within close range; at the fourth thrust, I'd pulled myself together and I grabbed him from behind and lashed out at his head four times, and since I was holding him so tight, he couldn't reach me to hit me; but he tried to protect himself with his arm and his sword, thinking this would do the trick, but as God would have it I struck him at the wrist, near the sleeve of his mail suit,

and swiped his hand clean off, and then gashed his head open. This last wound was more than enough: he begged me to leave him in one piece for the love of God. As I was pretty anxious to find out how Bebo had been getting on, I left him in the arms of a Venetian gent, who held him tightly so that he wouldn't try and jump in the canal.

When I turned round, I saw that Lorenzino was on his knees and struggling to his feet. I was pretty miffed and slashed out at his head, and chopped it in two. He fell full length at my feet, and didn't get up again.

I couldn't see where Bebo had got to; but if I wanted to scarper, I'd have to make for the church of San Marcello, where there's a small square, and here I found Bebo, looking like a total dope. I gently pointed out that the idea was actually for him to have come and given me a bit of a hand. When he tried to find an excuse I said, 'Now's not the time.' And so, keeping up a pretty smart pace, we'd soon left the arena of our little exploit far behind.

At the Santo Spirito ferry-landing, we decided it might be a good idea to chuck our daggers in the sea, so we did. Carrying daggers was banned, and you could get sent to the galleys for using them; but it wasn't to be long before I rather wished I'd never chucked my one away but held on to it. What happened was this: Bebo and I split, having agreed on a place to meet, since I was covered in blood, so that if I had the bad luck to be captured by the fuzz, he'd have a chance to escape. And hardly had Bebo left me when, turning round, who did I see but some twenty coppers on my trail. I immediately guessed they knew everything, and were coming to nab me; and to tell the truth, right then, I felt the game was up. Then, as quick as I could, I stepped out a bit and slipped into a church, and outside the church there was this group of people, and they all went in.

So down I knelt, and ardently commended myself to God, asking him to save and protect me. But all the time I was saying my prayers, I kept my eyes open, and I saw the whole crew of coppers cruising past – except one, who came into the church. I kept my eyes skinned, and looked backwards as well as forwards; and just then I'd have given anything for my dagger – being in a church wouldn't have stopped me. But I realised that they didn't actually know a thing, and so I bucked up, and decided I'd walk slap bang through the middle of those coppers, my mind made up to go into the church of Santo Spirito, where the Reverend Father Andrea da Volterra was preaching, and then slip out through the other door. But I couldn't do it for love nor money, there were so many people around. So I was forced to turn back; and one of those coppers came after me and followed me a fair way until I got to a crossroads. Then I pretended I had lost my way and turned back, and that copper just kept on following me, and I thought I must have roused his suspicions because I was all covered in blood. Then I pulled myself together, turned round and, much to his surprise, gave him such a wallop that he fell headlong; then I legged it as fast as I could.

I was dead beat by the time I reached the Flour Customs; so I headed off to San Marco and jumped into a gondola which took me to the Paglia Bridge, where the Albanesi house is. Here I spotted a man with a sword, and as it was a place where the cops stand guard during the daytime, my heart sank. So I went and knocked on the door of a tart who was a friend of mine; she recognised me and opened up immediately; but as I was going up, a little bird told me I shouldn't hang about here. So I thought I'd better go, and headed off again, and without my heart skipping a beat or being stopped by anyone I reached the house of my Lord the Count Selici da Collalto di

Friuli, a very dear and close pal of ours, since Bebo and me had been pretty useful to him in the past. I knocked on the door, and Bebo opened up straight away; and when he saw me spattered all over with blood, he was just amazed that I hadn't come to a sticky end and been pinched by the long arm of the law, as he'd been afraid must have happened when I'd taken so long getting there.

The Count wasn't at home, but since I was known to everyone in the household, I threw my weight around a bit, and went to the big fire in the kitchen, and used a bit of soap and water to make my white stockings nice and grey. Meantime, the Count arrived, and Bebo went up to him and they gave each other the glad hand and he asked after me. Then Bebo told him I'd had a bit of a run-in with a copper, all over a woman, and that he thought that I was really and truly dead. And while they were chatting about all this, up I pop and present myself to him as large as life. He gave me a nice warm welcome and we had a natter about this and that; and as we talked, dinner time was announced; but since the leading medic in Venice was coming to have dinner with him, the Count didn't want him to see us there, and in fact he didn't want any of his servants to see us either. So he ordered dinner to be served for us in a room upstairs, and he and his secretary served us at table, and he chattered away and had a bite to eat. Meanwhile, the aforesaid medic arrived, and the Count went off to have dinner with him; and the secretary stayed with us.

While they were washing their hands before sitting down to their meal, along came an embassy from Lorenzino's mother asking that, if the medic was here, could he go straight away over to her house, as Lorenzino had been killed and Alessandro Soderini was on his last legs. When he heard this, the medic left immediately, and didn't hang around to eat his

dinner; but the Count came up to us and asked us in no uncertain terms whether it had been us that had done it. We denied it till we were blue in the face, but he'd got it into his head that it *was* us. But he gave us a pep talk, telling us not to get the wind up, since he really wanted to do everything he could to protect us; but he knew that the problem was that he had to attend the council that day, and he didn't know what time he'd be going out, and so off he went to have his dinner, and then to have a nap.

When it was time for vespers I decided, without saying goodbye to anyone, to clear off; and I told Bebo to follow me and keep tabs on me from a distance, and if he saw me getting nabbed, he was to save his own skin as best he could. So off we went, and Bebo didn't know where I intended to go.

We went to the house of that lady where we'd first taken rooms, and I had supper ordered, thinking that I'd hang out here for a while and see if the news of our doings had spread, so as to take the appropriate measures. But meanwhile, who should come along but two priests, with that lady's son; those priests knew me, and so we started to have a chat about this and that. A little while later one of the priests went out; well, that made me think, and so I told that lady that I just had to pop out on an errand, and I'd be back soon; and I winked at Bebo to come with me and we went to the Maddalena landing and got into a gondola, telling the gondolier, 'Make it snappy!' and asking him to head off to Santa Maria Sobenighi; and when I reckoned we were in the middle of the canal, I told the boatman, 'Drop us off,' and I slipped him a few coins, telling him to wait till we got back. And as soon as we were on shore, near the palace of the Spanish ambassador, I told Bebo that what I had in mind was for us to take shelter there.[7]

This plan was rather to Bebo's liking, and he agreed

without further ado, and so we went into the palace of the said ambassador without anyone stopping us.

Once we were inside the palace, we found about forty Spaniards in there, all ready and waiting, and they treated us really politely, as if they'd heard all about the events and guessed that it was us; I didn't get flustered, and took no notice of them or all their glad-handing, but told them I urgently needed to talk with His Excellency the ambassador. One of those gents replied that His Excellency was not at home, but that he'd be back before long; so we started to stroll up and down in the courtyard for a quarter of an hour or so; then I said, 'My lords, since His Excellency hasn't shown up, we'll go and see to a little piece of business and come back later.' I didn't say this because I really wanted to leave, of course, but so they wouldn't think we were the ones they thought we were. Then one of them told us straight that if we didn't feel easy in the courtyard, we could go into a fine private room next door and settle down there and make ourselves comfortable, and that made me realise that they were thinking that we were not too keen on being seen. I told him that we couldn't care less about anyone seeing us, as we were decent, honourable chaps, and could show our faces anywhere in the world. So he went on, 'That's not why I made the suggestion, gentlemen, since everyone knows you're thoroughly decent fellows; but you ought to know that what made me ask was that this morning Lorenzino de' Medici was killed, and Alessandro Soderini was mortally wounded. Anyway, the one who survived said that there were two attackers: one of about twenty-eight, and the other thirty-one; one with white stockings, and the other man a bit on the sturdy side and well built. That's why I spoke the way I did. Don't let it bug you.' Then I told him we weren't those two; but since His

Excellency wasn't at home, we'd like a word or two with his esteemed secretary, and then we'd be off on our business.

They took us to the secretary straight away, and maybe thirty Spaniards came up behind us, all in a real merry state of excitement. When we got to the secretary's room, I started to say that we'd come to speak to His Excellency but since he wasn't at home, we'd very much like him, the secretary, to listen to what we had to say to His Excellency, and then we'd be on our way; but before we started talking, we'd very much prefer it if there weren't any other people around. So the secretary immediately got up from his desk, sent them all packing, and locked and bolted the door; then he gave us a really big welcome and made a huge fuss of us, even before I'd started talking, and told us we could speak perfectly openly, and without getting in a sweat. And so I gave him the low-down; and the minute I'd come to the end of my little story, he was just all over us, and told us he thought we were the bee's knees, as we'd done what loads of others had tried to do but never carried off. And then he shut us up in his room, telling us he was going to find His Excellency, as he knew just where he was. And off he went, but he was soon back, and through a secret winding staircase he led us into the room of His Excellency, who gave us yet another really warm and friendly reception before asking us to tell him once more how exactly we'd done the job. He sang our praises for all he was worth, and promised to use all the power and might of the Empire to make sure we were properly looked after and delivered safe and sound into the hands of the Duke of Florence[8].

'This very morning,' he continued, 'the minute I heard all about that fine and noble deed of yours, I sent off a messenger to the Emperor himself; and now I'm going to send off another one to tell him to guarantee you get well looked after and

protected by his forces. I'm telling you this because I know perfectly well he's going to be pleased as anything when he hears this news. So don't you worry about a thing; I hope to be getting orders very soon that will ensure you get a bit of proper protection.'

It wasn't ten days before we saw the result of His Excellency's efforts: a messenger came back with the answer that he was to do all in his power to protect us, and make sure he took prompt and swift action to get us back safe and sound into the hands of the Duke of Florence, as indeed happened.

Well, the prompt and swift action taken by His Excellency consisted in this: every morning he had it put about in the Rialto that the men who'd murdered Lorenzino had escaped to Padua on such and such a day; the next morning, he got people to say that on such and such a day they'd been spotted in Verona; other times, he'd have it announced that they'd been seen in Friuli, sometimes in one place, sometimes in another; and he did all this to dodge the numerous searches being carried out by the Florentines who'd been of Loren-zino's party, and the other rebels who were hanging out in Venice in great numbers and trying to get their hands on us. They'd posted guards at every entrance and exit, regardless of cost; what's more, they'd got four brigantines sailing up and down, keeping watch on all the passing gondolas; and His Excellency was well informed about all this, and kept his ears open for us.

Now, just you listen, and I'll tell you what great trouble His Excellency went to, to protect us.

He rented a really nice palace just outside where the Marghera passage is chained off, and every day he'd go there with fifty Spaniards; and when he was on shore, he'd take the carriages, and a group of them would head off on foot; it all

looked like an army, so those as had been posted to keep an eye on the Florentines all came over to see what was up, and every time they saw His Excellency, the minute he arrived, practising with his crossbow, and trotting round exercising a really nice horse; well, he ended up getting all those people so used to him that they no longer took any notice. Then, having calmed things down just as he wanted, he decided it was time to get us out of Venice, and he ordered the ambassador from Trent, Signor don Alberto of Spain, to come to Venice; then he handed the job over to him, and gave him a detailed description of us, giving him his orders on behalf of the Emperor and telling him how he was to deal with us and make sure we were safe and kept away from dangerous places, and where he was to arrange for post horses for us, and where we were to stop off, as you'll hear in a minute.

The day came when he thought it was the right time to get us out of Venice, and he sent up into our room his secretary, Signor Ximenes, to give us His Excellency's orders, which were to get ready to be off on our way; he gave us a long cassock down to our feet, and a short sword hanging from a belt, and a little cap and a big hat, so the two of us were dressed up like Brescians. Then he gave us a pair of scissors so we could cut off our beards, so that even someone who'd known us for donkey's years wouldn't ever have recognised us in these togs. Then we went down into His Excellency's room, and he made a huge big fuss of us all over again, and made us feel really welcome, and told us what schemes he'd been dreaming up on our behalf and what we needed to do if we were to get away in one piece. And after all this schmoozing he plopped down right in front of our eyes a big sack full of gold scudi, telling us to help ourselves to a good fifty, since we'd need them, as we had a really long journey ahead of us. As he

kept urging us, we took the money, and thanked him no end of times.

So we left the palace, and went to climb aboard a big gondola where there were twelve passengers all waiting, and a load of Spanish soldiers all tooled up – a good seventy of them. So off they went, and His Excellency set off too, and put us in his own gondola. So we headed off all bright and cheerful until we got to the Marghera port. When it was time to get out of the gondola, His Excellency jumped out first to see who was around; and who did he see but twenty-five Italian soldiers armed with harquebuses, standing around keeping an eye open for any Florentines who might be suspected of having carried out the job. While we stayed put in the gondola, waiting till the carriage was ready, they wanted to see who we were – so some of them wandered over and came up to our gondola to get a closer look. But His Excellency spotted what was going on and came back and asked those soldiers what the hell they thought they were up to and what they thought they were looking for, and he told them to clear off. So they did, pronto. Then His Excellency came to the gondola to tell us to get out, and he asked us if we were still feeling a bit feverish. Himself handed us into his carriage, and off we went to the palace he'd rented, with all his Spaniards leading the way; and as we were coming up to the palace, all the Spanish blokes went inside, and from the back door of the palace out came Captain Valeriano da Terni and his son with four post horses, two for us and two for them; and the ambassador gave us another hug and his very best wishes and said, 'You can go with these chaps to keep you company. They'll show you the road, and don't you worry about a thing.'

Then His Excellency went back into his palace, and we climbed onto the horses, and galloped off, from nine o'clock

till one in the morning, and kept the same horses till we got to a villa, where four fresh horses were waiting for us. We didn't have a bite to eat nor a drop to drink and didn't get a wink of sleep, just kept galloping on till it must have been six a.m. when we got to another villa, where we found a nice meal all ready, and new horses: and we reckoned then as we'd covered fifty miles. We stoked up, but still no shut-eye: back onto the horses it was, and this time we covered forty miles before stopping, so we'd got a good ninety miles all told away from Venice before we slept.

When we reached a fortified place where they spoke half German, we stopped in a hostelry, where mine host recognised us from the description His Excellency had sent him and realised we were in fact the people we were, and he gave us a real warm welcome and treated us better than if we'd been princes; and there we spent the night safe and sound, and the next morning at first peep we left with fresh half-post horses, so without needing to change them we galloped along till eight p.m., and reached some houses where there was a bailiff all ready and waiting for us, just as he'd been ordered to by a letter he'd already received. We had a snack and freshened up a bit and we were given new horses, and a guide, and for safety's sake he took us along out-of-the-way routes that nobody ever went down; and in three days he took us right through the territory of the King of the Romans, and then we headed for Trent.

When we reached there, we got off our horses outside a nice hostelry, and it wasn't long before two messengers came from Signor don Alberto, the local ambassador, telling us His Excellency was of a mind to have us stay with him. We were only too happy to do the right thing, so we followed instructions and didn't hang about but went and kowtowed to

His Excellency. We were thinking as how he wouldn't have heard about us or what had been happening (though in fact he knew every last little detail), so he kindly took us by the hand and told us he knew perfectly well who we were, and was fully up to date about the situation. Like he knew as how it had all happened in Venice, and it had been the idea of their protector the ambassador to have us brought here. We were gobsmacked. But he just kept making a fuss of us and praising us to the skies and insisting that we really must stay at his place, and he offered us cash up front and everything we needed. We said how very grateful we were and went back to our hostelry, where we had a bite to eat and then went off to sleep. And we slept like logs – we were bushwhacked.

Next morning, when we got up, we went over to pay our respects to His Excellency, and had a long chat with him about this and that, and he gave us a really nice breakfast. Then we let our guide and Captain Valeriano's son go, and they were only too pleased and went off, the guide back home and the other bloke to Venice. Then up trotted five post horses out of nowhere, as the ambassador wanted to come with us in person and keep us company till we got to the post station at Mantua. So as we wouldn't run into any danger, he sent five brave lads up ahead, to the town gate, where there were some German guards; he gave them express orders to make sure they stayed there, and if they started to get suspicious about us (which he didn't think would happen), or if they decided to get in our way, they were to lay into them until we'd got through. So we took to the open road. He made us change our horses the other side of the Adige, and as we'd got the wind up a bit we did a double stint. Anyway, we finally got to Mantua, safe and sound. We were about half a mile away when the ambassador split, telling us to stop at the Moor's Tavern, where we'd be

given a warm welcome. So we were – when we got there, mine host recognised us straight away, and I can't tell you what a fuss he made of us.

Then we went to pay our respects to My Lord the Cardinal of Mantua, who knew perfectly well who we were, and gave us cash, and some men to keep us company – in fact he wanted to give us fifty horsemen as far as Piacenza, just in case. But we humbly said thanks very much but no thank you, and went back to the tavern and got on our horses and reached Piacenza late that evening. Signor Don Diego di Mendoza was there, and we went to pay our respects, and to tell you the truth he was pretty chuffed to see us, and told us he'd let us have whatever we needed.

In the morning we left and went to a fortified place thirty miles away from Piacenza. The next day we got to Borgo Val di Taro, where there's a fortress held by the Emperor's men, and inside it there was one Captain Francesco Anguscioli, a gent from Piacenza. He went on and on trying to get us to stay in his fortress with him, but we refused, though we told him as how we were deeply grateful for the offer. But next morning he came over in person at first peep to see us, and took us to his fortress, and gave us a breakfast fit for a king rather than for blokes such as us. Anyway, that night at two o'clock there arrived at the tavern where we were staying a man of about thirty, on horseback, all kitted out with a chain-mail jacket and sleeves, and a dirty great wheel-lock harquebus and two smaller versions, short-barrelled pistols in fact. So mine host asked him where he was coming from and where he was going to, and he said he'd come that same day from Piacenza and was off to Pontremoli on a piece of business. We really got the wind up at this, especially as he left before the crack of dawn. We had a word in the ear of the captain in charge of that

fortress I mentioned, and he didn't hang about but sent off two soldiers on fine steeds with nice fine weapons, telling them in no uncertain terms to get their horses going at a cracking pace till they caught up with the bloke I mentioned just now and just make sure they brought him back, by force if necessary. And if he didn't want to come quietly, or if he put up a fight, they should do the necessary on him.

The two of them took off straight away and before long they'd caught up with him, as he was only trotting along. He came quiet as you please and they brought him to the captain, who locked him in the slammer. We later heard as how he sent him to Don Diego in Piacenza, and no one knows what became of him after that. But I'll tell you this for a certain fact: he'd been sent to do us a mischief. But thanks to our captain he blew it. Anyway, we left town, and that evening got to Pontremoli, where the man in charge of the castle there gave us a nice warm welcome. In the morning we got on our horses and rode off with the post and the postilion. The roads were lousy so we thought we'd not make Pisa by nightfall, especially as Captain Valeriano, who'd been travelling with us ever since Venice, was an old-timer who was dead beat by now, since we'd been riding for thirteen days at a stretch. We decided we'd leave him to it, and he could make it to Pisa at his own speed, as he did. We galloped off at top speed and got to Pisa at four a.m., and found the Duke there sitting down to a nice supper.

There was a general agreement that we shouldn't have a proper audience just then as it was so late. So we went to an inn and ordered some supper, and then we went to get some shut-eye, and next morning we went to have an audience with him.

As soon as we were in the presence of the Duke, he made a real fuss over us, and gave us the warmest welcome, and

praised us to the skies. He insisted on hearing again from my own lips (although he already knew all about it through the letters he'd received) how the job had been carried out. I was all too happy to obey, in fact that was only ever what I wanted, so I told him as best I could. Then he told us what good chaps we were and praised us no end, and said what brave lads we'd been, and how he himself was really most obliged to us, and wouldn't forget. Then he went on to tell us that we would be safe anywhere in his territory, and he issued a pardon for our wrongdoings, with detailed letters and privileges, telling us in no uncertain terms that we were to be given our just deserts not only by him personally but by his whole household too. He promised us all these privileges would be observed without fail, and they were, too.

The Duke went even further, in fact, and gave us a pension and a nice little income to keep body and soul together – quite a tidy sum, all told, and certainly enough for us to spend the rest of our lives in splendid style, with not a care in the world.

Bebo, a bit later, I misremember exactly when, went off to Volterra, where he was from, and ended his days there. And I stayed in Florence. No more war for me: I just wanted to live my life in blessed peace and quiet.

NOTES

1. i.e. Cosimo I.

2. The Italian phrase used by Bebo is rather more specific: '*cavaliere errante*', or 'knight-errant'.

3. The distinguished Strozzi family had mostly gone into exile from Florence and continued to plot against Cosimo. Piero Strozzi (1510–58), mentioned later as a protector of Lorenzino, was son of the celebrated Filippo (1489–1538). Piero had led the rebels to defeat at Montemurlo in 1537.

4. Giovanni della Casa (1503–56) was not only a papal functionary, but a man of letters whose *Galateo* (1558) became a widely known treatise on good manners.

5. Elena Barozza was a famous courtesan, painted by (among others) Titian and praised for her beauty by Aretino.

6. Bibboni's knife seems to have been poisoned. Alessandro Soderini died of his wounds. The exact location of the murder is not entirely clear from Bibboni's account, but probably took place near the San Tomè bridge.

7. The Spanish embassy would have been a safe haven for Bibboni, given the Spanish Emperor Charles V's support for Cosimo and hostility to Lorenzino.

8. i.e. Cosimo.

Poems by Lorenzino de' Medici

Translated by J.G. Nichols

To the Emperor Charles V *

After showing such evil enterprise,
O Caesar, such worldwide rapacity –
Far races robbed and in captivity
So many times, both friends and enemies,

All Africa laid waste, your forces hurled
Against lands in the West, once you had won
Our Europe, leaving nothing to be done
To ruin every country in the world

But go against the East and, making head
Against the sun, keep thieving – now at last,
Eagle returning to your origin,

What can you say, with land and sea laid waste,
But, like a thief with no respect for God:
'My Lord, I've stolen all the sun shines on.'

* This sonnet is a parody of an adulatory sonnet written by the 'establishment' poet
Annibal Caro (1507–66). Lorenzino's attack on the Emperor is probably meant to
corroborate the idea that fierce anti-tyrannical feelings prompted him to kill his
cousin, the Duke Alessandro de' Medici.

The more I plough the Adriatic Sea…

The more I plough the Adriatic Sea,
The more I move towards the rising sun,
So much the more desire flies back again,
To be where that sun hides itself away;

So, if I have a favourable wind
From Him no one adores sufficiently,
My soul will soon be where it wants to be,
And I shall reach the ocean's utmost bound.

But not by change of season or of place
Does my just fierce desire abandon me,
Indeed it does my soul more injuries:

My soul at parting called it cowardice
To flee to folk who are so far away,
Abandoning its glorious enterprise.

*When I look at the flaming East, and see**

When I look at the flaming East, and see
The sun rise with the day and lovely dawn,
I tell myself that quickening sun has seen
My beloved brothers only recently.

And then I have this kindly, foolish thought:
Could I be in the gleaming chariot when
With its immortal rays it gilds the town
By the base Arno that had once such might!

An honest flame of love inflames my heart,
Because I never left you, glad to leave.
Nor do I hope to live in separation.

That other thing, the world calls love, is not.
Transferring one's affections makes one grieve
At last for having such a foolish notion.

* After the assassination of Alessandro de' Medici, Lorenzino embarked on a series
of travels through Italy and then abroad (see note 13 to the *Apology*).

Madrigal

Hell burns within my breast;
My soul's a hellish soul;
The fire in which I burn is fire from hell.
I burn; no hope, no rest.
I have for ever lost
The sight of one loved most.
To me one wish is all.
One thing makes different
My lot from that of the forsaken nation –
They burn with reason: I am innocent.
They often curse and hate
The God responsible for their creation:
I praise and love the one who makes my fire so hot.

Lorenzino de' Medici was born in 1514 to Pierfrancesco, from the cadet branch of the Medici family, and Maria Soderini. Born Lorenzo, he was later called Lorenzino, perhaps to differentiate him from his illustrious ancestors and for his weak constitution. After spending his youth in Rome under the guardianship of Pope Clement VII (the illegitimate son of Lorenzo the Magnificent's brother), he was forced to repair to Florence, having vandalised, during a drunken spree, the bas-reliefs on the Emperor Constantine's triumphal arch and the statues of the Muses in the basilica of San Paolo. There he befriended his distant cousin Alessandro who had become the Duke of Florence two years previously in 1531. Lorenzino became the Duke's companion in debauchery and their conduct became notorious throughout the city. During this time of dissipation he wrote a comedy, *Aridosio*, in honour of Alessandro's wedding. In January 1537 Lorenzino hatched a plan to kill his cousin, allegedly – as he would later explain in his *Apology* – to free Florence from his tyrannical rule. The real motives of his murder, though, remain a mystery. After the assassination, Lorenzino embarked on a series of journeys across Italy and then abroad, in search of support against the reinstated Medici Duke. Having travelled extensively for many years, he returned to Venice, where he became acquainted with the higher echelons of refined Venetian society, including Giovanni della Casa, the author of the celebrated *Galateo*, and the famous courtesan Elena Barozza. It was on a visit to her in 1548 that he was finally tracked down by the Duke of Florence's hired assassins, and was killed.

Andrew Brown studied at the University of Cambridge, where he taught French for many years. He now works as a freelance teacher and translator. He is the author of *Roland Barthes: The Figures of Writing* (OUP, 1993), and his translations include *Memoirs of a Madman* by Gustave Flaubert, *For a Night of Love* by Emile Zola, *The Jinx* by Théophile Gautier, *Mademoiselle de Scudéri* by E.T.A Hoffmann, *Theseus* by André Gide, *Incest* by Marquis de Sade, *The Ghost-seer* by Friedrich von Schiller, *Colonel Chabert* by Honoré de Balzac, *Memoirs of an Egotist* by Stendhal, *Butterball* by Guy de Maupassant, *With the Flow* by Joris-Karl Huysmans, and *Manon Lescaut* by Antoine François Prévost, all published by Hesperus Press.

HESPERUS PRESS CLASSICS

Hesperus Press, as suggested by the Latin motto, is committed to bringing near what is far – far both in space and time. Works written by the greatest authors, and unjustly neglected or simply little known in the English-speaking world, are made accessible through new translations and a completely fresh editorial approach. Through these classic works, the reader is introduced to the greatest writers from all times and all cultures.

For more information on Hesperus Press, please visit our website: **www.hesperuspress.com**

ET REMOTISSIMA PROPE

SELECTED TITLES FROM HESPERUS PRESS

Author	Title	Foreword writer
Louisa May Alcott	*Behind a Mask*	Doris Lessing
Pedro Antonio de Alarcon	*The Three-Cornered Hat*	
Pietro Aretino	*The School of Whoredom*	Paul Bailey
Jane Austen	*Love and Friendship*	Fay Weldon
Honoré de Balzac	*Colonel Chabert*	A.N. Wilson
Charles Baudelaire	*On Wine and Hashish*	Margaret Drabble
Aphra Behn	*The Lover's Watch*	
Giovanni Boccaccio	*Life of Dante*	A.N. Wilson
Charlotte Brontë	*The Green Dwarf*	Libby Purves
Mikhail Bulgakov	*The Fatal Eggs*	Doris Lessing
Giacomo Casanova	*The Duel*	Tim Parks
Miguel de Cervantes	*The Dialogue of the Dogs*	
Anton Chekhov	*The Story of a Nobody*	Louis de Bernières
Anton Chekhov	*Three Years*	William Fiennes
Wilkie Collins	*Who Killed Zebedee?*	Martin Jarvis
Arthur Conan Doyle	*The Tragedy of the Korosko*	Tony Robinson
William Congreve	*Incognita*	Peter Ackroyd
Joseph Conrad	*Heart of Darkness*	A.N. Wilson
Joseph Conrad	*The Return*	Colm Tóibín
Gabriele D'Annunzio	*The Book of the Virgins*	Tim Parks
Dante Alighieri	*New Life*	Louis de Bernières
Daniel Defoe	*The King of Pirates*	Peter Ackroyd
Marquis de Sade	*Incest*	Janet Street-Porter
Charles Dickens	*The Haunted House*	Peter Ackroyd
Charles Dickens	*A House to Let*	
Fyodor Dostoevsky	*The Double*	Jeremy Dyson
Fyodor Dostoevsky	*Poor People*	Charlotte Hobson
Joseph von Eichendorff	*Life of a Good-for-nothing*	